BELIEVE

Published in 2022 by OH!
An Imprint of Welbeck Non-Fiction Limited,
part of Welbeck Publishing Group.
Based in London and Sydney.
www.welbeckpublishing.com

Compilation text © Welbeck Non-Fiction Limited 2022
Design © Welbeck Non-Fiction Limited 2022

ISBN 978-1-80069-233-6

Compilation, writing, design: RH
Editorial: Lisa Dyer
Project manager: Russell Porter
Production: Jess Brisley

A CIP catalogue record for this book is available from the British Library

Printed in China

10 9 8 7 6 5 4 3 2

Illustrations: shutterstock.com

BELIEVE

THE LITTLE GUIDE TO
TED LASSO

CONTENTS

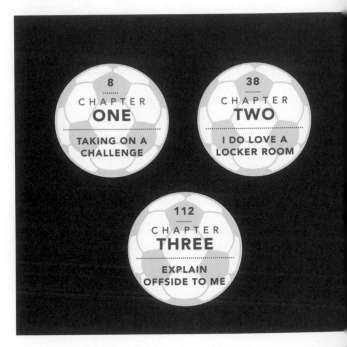

INTRODUCTION

The phenomenon that is Apple TV+'s *Ted Lasso* is not going away any time soon; this is for all time. Highly original and super funny, the show about an American coach who comes to England to run a Premier League soccer (football to the Brits) team has caught the hearts and minds of television watchers around the world—as well as the eye of numerous critics and prize-givers.

Perhaps it is the feel-good nature of the show and its timing that has seen it win Grammy awards aplenty, as well as many others (*Ted Lasso* broke the record for the number of nominations for a comedy series). But it's more likely that such a funny, sharply scripted, brilliantly delivered comedy of manners, nationality, rationality, love, relationships, and inspiration about people who are fundamentally decent and willing to help others has mass appeal, and more than earned its critical and popular acclaim.

Headlined by Jason Sudeikis in the titular role and with a mega-watt talented ensemble cast that includes fellow Emmy-winners Brett Goldstein as Roy and Hannah Waddingham as Rebecca, the show racked up seven Emmys in 2021 alone.

This little book reveals what exactly the writers, cast, and characters wanted to say when they blew the whistle of creativity on the show. The way it tackles feelings, relationships, mental health in sport (and in general), personal goals, and crises—there's so much packed in to those neat episodes with their ever-expanding, bittersweet storylines.

Here you'll find amusing and interesting quotes, including some of the classic one-liners from Ted and the rest of the brilliant cast, as well as fun facts and stats about the actors, writers, AFC Richmond, and more … So let's quit goofing around and get on with it … Whistle! *Whistle!*

CHAPTER

1

TAKING ON A CHALLENGE

Ted Lasso and Coach Beard (we still don't know if that is a name or a description) come to England to coach AFC Richmond, a made-up team who play in a real stadium (Selhurst Park, since you ask).

Ted has personal issues, the team is in disarray, and it turns out he's being set up to fail. But how did this complicated backstory come to pass? This chapter discusses the origins of Ted Lasso and his meteoric rise to greatness.

TED LASSO, THE EARLY YEARS

The character Ted Lasso first appeared in a series of short NBC Sports promos featuring Jason Sudeikis in 2013. They were used for NBC Sports' coverage of the U.K.'s Premier League, under the title "An American Coach in London."

The club Lasso took charge of was "The Tottenham Hotspurs."

BELIEVE

"

Jason brought to this a desire to make this show that's dedicated to that seminal teacher or coach or relative or friend figure that was a true mentor in every sense of the word.

"

Bill Lawrence (co-creator) on Jason Sudeikis's inspiration for Ted Lasso.

Source: Bill Lawrence interview with Josh Jackson, *Paste*, October 2, 2020, pastemagazine.com

---

In an effort to infuse some American culture into soccer, they hired Jason Sudeikis for a TV spot where he played Lasso: a distinctly American football coach who was mistakenly hired to coach the Tottenham Hotspurs.

Critic **Arul Gnanasivam** *on the origins of the Ted Lasso character.*

Source: "The History of Ted Lasso" by Arul Gnanasivam, DBK News, September 22, 2021, dbknews.com

BELIEVE

66

So, one day in 2015, my partner
Olivia [Wilde] came up to me and
said, 'You know, you should do
Ted Lasso as a show.'

99

Jason Sudeikis on *Ted Lasso's evolution.*

Source: Quoted in article by Luis Miguel Echegaray,
Sports Illustrated, August 11, 2020, si.com

"

I'd seen those sketches and I thought they were broad and funny, but they were sketch. **"**

*Co-creator **Bill Lawrence** on the early Ted Lasso incarnations.*

Source: Bill Lawrence interview with Josh Jackson, *Paste*, October 2, 2020, pastemagazine.com

THE REAL AFC RICHMOND

- *Ted Lasso* is filmed at Selhurst Park in Croydon, London. It is home to Crystal Palace FC, who play in red and blue.

- Ted's apartment is on Paved Court in Richmond, London.

- The Crown & Anchor is actually The Prince's Head, a real pub on the edge of Richmond Green.

The bulk of my soccer knowledge and love comes from playing 'FIFA.'

Jason Sudeikis reveals how he learned about the beautiful game.

Source: Jason Sudeikis interview with Kevin Baxter, *Los Angeles Times*, August 14, 2020, latimes.com

BELIEVE

66

The whole story of that first commercial was that he gets hired to coach a professional soccer team and he gets fired three days later, and we just thought it would be funny if he wasn't cynical or angry about that, that he just loved the experience …

99

Jason Sudeikis on the earliest iteration of Ted Lasso.

Source: Interview with Derek Lawrence in *Entertainment Weekly*, August 13, 2020, ew.com

---

Bill writes male characters and relationships so beautifully, his use of music and dealing with heavy duty issues of life and death. And now, two years later, here we are talking about it.

Jason Sudeikis on Bill Lawrence.

Source: Article by Luis Miguel Echegaray, *Sports Illustrated*, August 11, 2020, si.com

BELIEVE

❝

They had like four or five ideas and one of them was an American coach coaching soccer in London ... more of a yelling, screaming, kind of Bobby Knight drill sergeant vibe ... I just saw something a little bit different, and that is what ended up becoming Ted Lasso.

❞

Jason Sudeikis on how Ted's character began to evolve.

Source: Interview with Derek Lawrence in *Entertainment Weekly*, August 13, 2020, ew.com

66

That's where the moustache
comes from.

99

*Jason Sudeikis on what his father
contributed to the character of Ted Lasso.*

Source: Interview on *The Today Show*,
July 22, 2021, youtube.com

BELIEVE

"

So, we sat down, and we were able to bang out a pilot pretty quick in that week. As well as outlining six to ten episodes of the first season.

"

Jason Sudeikis *on first writing.*

Source: Article by Luis Miguel Echegaray, *Sports Illustrated,*
August 11, 2020, si.com

… but why would he take this job? Why would a guy at this age take this job to leave? Maybe he's having marital strife. Maybe things aren't good back home, so he needs space.

Jason Sudeikis *ponders Ted's motivation.*

Source: Interview with Zach Baron in *GQ*, July 13, 2021, gq.com

BELIEVE

"

At this point, I have a deep appreciation for the sport but still a very shallow understanding. **"**

Jason Sudeikis *on his knowledge of soccer.*

Source: Interview with Derek Lawrence, *Entertainment Weekly*, August 13, 2021, ew.com

---

Ted Lasso originated even before the NBC primer spots. Sudeikis actually helped create the character in 2001 while performing comedy with show co-star Brendan Hunt.

*Critic **Arul Gnanasivam** sheds new light on Ted's earliest origins.*

Source: "The History of Ted Lasso" by Arul Gnanasivam, DBK News, September 22, 2021, dbknews.com

BELIEVE

He created this character, Ted Lasso, and made some wonderful comedy out of this dimwit American dropping into the English soccer scene.

Critic **Esther Walker**.

Source: "Ted Lasso: Why?" by Esther Walker, *The Spike*, 2021, onthespike.com

I've been friends with Jason for seven years … we stayed in touch. When I moved to L.A., I saw him at a play. And [he told me], 'Oh, I'm filming this TV show soon in London and it'd be cool to have you.'

Moe Jeudy-Lamour *on how he joined the* Ted Lasso *cast.*

Source: Interview with Emily Burack, *Alma*,
September 17, 2021, heyalma.com

BELIEVE

66

It all started with the purchase of a Playstation in 2001. Sudeikis bought the system while living in the Netherlands and working for the confusingly named Boom Chicago, an American comedy troupe in the Netherlands.

99

Grant Marek on Ted Lasso's origins.

Source: Grant Marek, SFGATE, August 2, 2021, sfgate.com

Three, four nights a week, especially over the last few months, me, other writers, and cast members are playing on FIFA Pro Clubs.

Jason Sudeikis on how video games helped the show's evolution.

Source: Interview with Derek Lawrence, *Entertainment Weekly*, August 13, 2021, ew.com

BELIEVE

"

I think we've always meant it to be three seasons.

"

Brendan Hunt *(co-creator and co-star) on the longevity of* Ted Lasso.

Source: Interview with Clark Collis, *Entertainment Weekly*, June 8, 2021, ew.com

It is a locker room vibe, because everybody there is football crazy. And some of the cast who weren't football crazy are now football crazy.

Kola Bokinni *on living the dream while filming with the crew on* Ted Lasso.

Source: Article by Meredith B. Kile in ET, October 8, 2021, etonline.com

ART IMITATES LIFE

English football club Chester City FC had American football coach Terry Smith as manager following a takeover in 1999. He claimed, "All coaching is 90 percent the same, regardless of the sport."

His tenure saw the club relegated.

Source: "The Madness of Terry Smith: Chester City's American Nightmare" by Sean Makin, *Football Pink*, August 9, 2020, footballpink.net

HANDS IN THE AIR

The *Ted Lasso* theme tune is performed by Marcus Mumford, of Mumford & Sons, and was written by him and Tom Howe.

Jason Sudeikis appeared in the video for "Hopeless Wanderer" in 2013.

BELIEVE

66

We felt the theme song had to
be placed somewhere right in the
middle of the Atlantic, between
the U.K. and the U.S.

99

Jason Sudeikis *on* Ted Lasso's *theme tune.*

Source: *The Hollywood Reporter*, quoted by Nicholas
DeRenzo, AARP, July 20, 2021, aarp.org

You gotta start from Jason. Most people know Jason as an actor, but he was a *writer* on *SNL* first.

Bill Lawrence *on Jason Sudeikis.*

Source: Bill Lawrence interview with Josh Jackson, *Paste*, October 2, 2020, pastemagazine.com

THE LAD'S GOT FORM

The show's co-creator, Bill Lawrence, was also instrumental in the creation of classics *Spin City*, *Scrubs*, *Cougar Town* and *The Nanny*.

66

There's a warmth and an earnestness to Coach Lasso that on paper should come across as phony, saccharine, emotionally manipulative. Instead it's a strange reminder of human dignity and human decency.

99

Bill Lawrence *on the depth of Ted's character.*

Source: Bill Lawrence interview with Josh Jackson, *Paste*, October 2, 2020, pastemagazine.com

BELIEVE

"

When I heard about him taking his squad to go do karaoke, I was like, 'hellooooo, story idea …'

"

Jason Sudeikis *on Liverpool FC manager Jurgen Klopp's influence on Ted.*

Source: Article by Luis Miguel Echegaray, *Sports Illustrated*, August 11, 2020, si.com

---

CHAPTER

2

I DO LOVE A LOCKER ROOM

Ted Lasso has brilliant characters. A seemingly random, international group of talented oddballs has come together to make a show that is even better than its already hugely talented constituent parts.

The storylines are human, moving, touching, funny, rude, and topical, and they are played to perfection by the superb cast ...

TED LASSO
(Jason Sudeikis)

Jason was born in 1975 in Viriginia and works as a producer, writer, and comedian as well as an actor.

He was a writer and performer on *Saturday Night Live*, as well as *30 Rock*, *It's Always Sunny in Philadelphia*, *Portlandia*, and *The Last Man on Earth* before *Ted Lasso*.

BELIEVE

66

It's up to me to not just play an a-hole in every movie.

99

Jason Sudeikis *on his fear of being typecast.*

Source: Interview with Zach Baron in *GQ*,
July 13, 2021, gq.com

REBECCA WELTON

(Hannah Waddingham)

Born in 1975 in London, Rebecca is a theatrical and big- and small-screen actress. She is a regular on TV and has appeared in *Game of Thrones*, *Benidorm*, *Sex Education*, and *Midsomer Murders* as well as in movies and West End theater.

She has been nominated for three Olivier awards for her stage work.

BELIEVE

"

The writers have moved her on in terms of work and how you see her relationships with the players, but she's a hot mess with men, and I love that.

"

Hannah Waddingham *on Rebecca Welton's character development.*

Source: Interview with Caroline Hallemann in *Town & Country*, July 23, 2021, townandcountrymag.com

---

66

That Rebecca is an intimidating and very tall woman.

99

Keeley Jones *on her new boss at*
AFC Richmond.

Source: Quoted by Katie Bowlby, *Country Living*,
August 24, 2021, countryliving.com

BELIEVE

I had already decided for myself that Rebecca has probably mostly —and in her head totally—missed the boat at the chance of being a mother naturally. **99**

Hannah Waddingham *on Rebecca's thoughts on parenthood.*

Source: Interview with Saloni Gajjar, *AV Club*, September 8, 2021, avclub.com

Yeah, you have the bad owner who just wants to destroy the team, but instead of just doing that trope you go, 'Hey, how'd she get there?' Maybe you empathize for a bit.

Bill Lawrence *on sympathy for and understanding of Rebecca Welton.*

Source: Bill Lawrence interview with Josh Jackson, *Paste*, October 2, 2020, pastemagazine.com

BELIEVE

66

Boss, I tell you, I'd hate to see you and Michelle Obama arm wrestle, but I wouldn't be able take my eyes off of it either. **99**

Ted Lasso on his new boss at AFC Richmond.

Source: Quoted by Katie Bowlby, *Country Living*, August 24, 2021, countryliving.com

---

LESLIE HIGGINS

(Jeremy Swift)

Swift was born in Stockton-on-Tees, England, in 1960 and has been a regular in movies and on TV for many years.

He has appeared in *Downton Abbey*, *Mary Poppins Returns*, *Gosford Park*, *Jupiter Ascending*, *Doctors*, *Wanderlust*, *Foyle's War*, and *The Crimson Field*, among many others.

BELIEVE

66

I'm *very* British. I can't quite deal with the Emmy thing, to be honest.

99

Jeremy Swift on the (many) awards that Ted Lasso *picked up.*

Source: Interview with Lesley O'Toole in the *Los Angeles Times*, August 10, 2021, latimes.com

Higgins is coming from a good place. He's not one of the more toxic male characters in the show. So I just used my sense of smell to figure out where he was going!

Jeremy Swift *on his character Higgins.*

Source: Interview with Anthony Breznican in *Vanity Fair*, August 13, 2021, vanityfair.com

JAMIE TARTT
(Phil Dunster)

Phil Dunster was born in Reading, England, in 1992. He is a regular actor on screens big and small, including *Murder on the Orient Express*, *The Trouble with Maggie Cole*, *Strike Back*, *Save Me* and *Humans*. IRL he is a fan of AFC Wimbledon.

With Brett, we have been very fortunate in that we've become very good friends, and he knew this was a big scene for me and for Jamie.

Phil Dunster on Jamie Tartt's key big-hug scene with Roy Kent.

Source: Interview with Alicia Lutes in *Vulture*, September 10, 2021, vulture.com

BELIEVE

How Jamie Tartt came to be Jamie Tartt was that he was originally Dani Rojas.

Phil Dunster *reveals that Jamie Tartt was not the character he originally auditioned for in* Ted Lasso.

Source: Interview with Caroline Hallemann in *Town & Country*, August 31, 2021, townandcountrymag.com

"

Me!

"

Jamie Tartt shows his ego to the AFC Richmond crowd as they sing his name.

Source: Quoted in "When a Show about Kindness Gets Darker" by Megan Garber, *The Atlantic*, July 23, 2021, theatlantic.com

BELIEVE

66

Freud would have an absolute
field day with him.

99

Phil Dunster on his character Jamie Tartt.

Source: Interview with Alicia Lutes in *Vulture*,
September 10, 2021, vulture.com

ROY KENT
(Brett Goldstein)

A writer, actor, and stand-up comedian, Brett was born in 1980 in Sutton, England. In addition to writing for *Ted Lasso*, he wrote for *The Catherine Tate Show* in 2016.

He acted in *Hoff the Record*, *Catherine Tate's Mum*, *Soulmates*, and *Undercover*, and has been in an episode of *Doctor Who*.

Roy Kent is loosely based on the Manchester United and Republic of Ireland footballer Roy Keane.

BELIEVE

66

I understood the sadness of that.
I understood his depression.
And, most of all, I fully understood
the rage.

99

*Brett on Roy's injury that forces his
retirement from playing.*

Source: Interview with Emily Zemler in *Rolling Stone*,
August 20, 2021, rollingstone.com

66

Oi! If I don't hear silence, I'm gonna start punching dicks!

99

*Captain **Roy Kent** gets the dressing room to shut up.*

Source: Quoted in *Ted Lasso* review, *Entertainment Weekly*, August 3, 2021, ew.com

---

BELIEVE

"

There were a million different ways Roy could have turned out, but Jason has a very good rule of look at the script, look at the characters, and the answer is almost always there.

"

Brett Goldstein *on Jason Sudeikis's methods and Roy's character development.*

Source: Interview with Joanna Robinson, *Vanity Fair*, August 20, 2021, vanityfair.com

---

COACH BEARD
(Brendan Hunt)

Brendan Hunt is co-creator and writer of *Ted Lasso* as well as being a cast member.

Brendan was born in 1972 in Chicago and has been an actor and writer since 1999. He has worked with Jason Sudeikis on *Horrible Bosses 2*, *We're the Millers*, and *Saturday Night Live*.

We suspect that nobody—even Brendan—knows if Coach Beard is the character's actual name.

BELIEVE

❝

What's fun about him is how
mysterious he is.

❞

Brendan Hunt *on Coach Beard.*

Source: Anthony Breznican in *Vanity Fair*,
July 30, 2021, vanityfair.com

But Ted's world view isn't a delusion, it's a choice. What rattles everyone—the show's characters and us watching at home—is the realization that we have that choice, too.

Brendan Hunt on the finer points of Ted Lasso's character.

Source: Interview with Kevin Fallon, *The Daily Beast*, July 30, 2021, thedailybeast.com

BELIEVE

The true appeal of Coach Beard is in the negative space he creates: what we don't know, can't see, and maybe can't even imagine about him.

Brendan Hunt *explains the intricacies of Coach Beard's character.*

Source: Anthony Breznican in *Vanity Fair*, July 30, 2021, vanityfair.com

NATHAN "NATE" SHELLEY

(Nick Mohammad)

Nick was born in Leeds, England, in 1980. He is a regular on television screens as well as the radio.

His credits include *The Job Lot*, *Fresh Meat*, *Hitmen*, and *Inside No. 9*. His radio shows *Nick Mohammed in Bits* and *Detective Sergeant Nick Mohammed* are very popular and received much critical acclaim.

BELIEVE

" What's interesting now is this is a character who still has the same demons and insecurities, but he's now got this position of power. **"**

Nick Mohammad *on what makes Nate tick.*

Source: Interview with Mandi Kerr on Showbiz Cheat Sheet, September 2, 2021, cheatsheet.com

My most enduring hope is that next year's Emmy voters recognize that as much as we all love Roy Kent, Mohammed deserves serious consideration.

Sandra Gonzalez *for CNN on the great "Nate Debate."*

Source: Sandra Gonzalez, CNN, October 8, 2021, edition.cnn.com

KEELEY JONES
(Juno Temple)

Juno has been appearing on TV and movie screens for many years. Her most famous parts include Lola Quincey in *Atonement*, a good fairy in *Maleficent*, Fanny Robin in *Far from the Madding Crowd*, and Jamie Vine in HBO's *Vinyl*.

Juno was born in London in 1989 and her first screen role was in 2000, in *Pandaemonium*.

Keeley Jones is the glue that holds all the different components of Apple TV+'s heartwarming sports comedy *Ted Lasso* together.

Eric Betts *is firmly behind Keeley as a key character.*

Source: Article in *Looper*, August 6, 2021, looper.com

BELIEVE

"

I'm sort of famous for being almost famous.

"

Keeley Jones comments on Keeley Jones, *the ultimate WAG.*

Source: Quoted by Katie Bowlby, *Country Living*, August 24, 2021, countryliving.com

---

Keeley's strength lies in her kindness. Her vivacious spirit. She's proof positive that women can be strong in a myriad of ways. You can be benevolent while still setting boundaries and defending yourself when it's needed.

Melodie McCune, *Geek Girl Authority Crush of the Week: Keeley Jones.*

Source: Geek Girl Authority, September 1, 2021, geekgirlauthority.com

BELIEVE

"

I've done karaoke with her. I've been in a room with her. I knew her. She's so fun and dynamic and just pro-female. She's just a kick-ass that lives with an excitement that's fun to be around, and that's a little bit of what the character had.

"

Jason Sudeikis on what makes Juno Temple and Keeley Jones.

Source: Article by Luis Miguel Echegaray, *Sports Illustrated*, August 11, 2020, si.com

DR. SHARON FIELDSTONE
(Sarah Niles)

Sarah is an actress for television, film, and theater. On the small screen, she was in *Beautiful People*, *Catastrophe*, and *I May Destroy You*.

Her numerous theatrical appearances include *Anthony and Cleopatra* and *The Crucible*, and movies include *Rocks* and *Happy-Go-Lucky*.

BELIEVE

66

I think Dr. Sharon is very ambitious and she's got a kind heart. She's very good at her job. She wants the best for everyone. **99**

Sarah Niles on the character and motivation of Dr. Sharon.

Source: Interview with Meaghan Darwish in *TV Insider*, August 4, 2021, tvinsider.com

---

So I watched the show and I was like, 'This is really good! It's really what I need right now.'

Sarah Niles on Ted Lasso's *quality and positive message.*

Source: Interview with Christopher Orr in the *New York Times*, July 30, 2021, nytimes.com

BELIEVE

> There's a wonderful atmosphere here, all the employees are thoughtful and kind, and they actually listen to one another.

Dr. Sharon Fieldstone's original assessment of the AFC Richmond.

Source: Quoted in "When a Show about Kindness Gets Darker" by Megan Garber, *The Atlantic*, July 23, 2021, theatlantic.com

SAM OBISANYA

(Toheeb Jimoh)

Toheeb Jimoh was born in 1997 in England. Both of his parents are of Nigerian descent—just like Sam—and Toheeb did spend time in Nigeria as a child. He was in *Anthony* on BBC1 in 2020 and the Amazon series *The Feed*.

The character of Sam was originally from Ghana, but was changed by the writers to Nigeria when Toheeb got on board.

BELIEVE

"

He quotes Rainer Maria Rilke, unironically claims *Ratatouille* as his favorite film, and doesn't suffer from a chronic case of dumpster mouth. **"**

*Critic **Melanie McFarland** on the hidden depths of character Sam Obisanya.*

Source: Interview with Melanie McFarland in *Salon*, September 25, 2021, salon.com

I have a lot of people, a lot of Nigerian people, on my Instagram and on my Twitter who reach out and just say that they feel seen because of the episode.

Toheeb Jimoh *on fan reaction to his political stance.*

Source: Interview with Melanie McFarland in *Salon*, September 25, 2021, salon.com

BELIEVE

66

Do you mind if I don't keep this?
I don't have the same fondness for
the American military that you do.

99

Sam Obisanya's politics are apparent, from
his reaction to Ted's gift of a plastic soldier.

Source: Quoted in interview with Toheeb Jimoh by Karenna
Meredith, Popsugar, August 31, 2021, popsugar.co.uk

Rebecca: Sam . . . you're so kind and loving and wise. But . . . there's just this one issue that I can't get past.
Sam: What is it?
Rebecca: You're wonderful.

Rebecca's "Let's take a break" chat with Sam doesn't follow the usual protocols.

Source: Quoted in Melanie McFarland interview in *Salon*, September 25, 2021, salon.com

BELIEVE

❝

I love Sam Obisanya. I know, he's a fictional character, but the world could use more footballers like Sam.

❞

*Critic **Travis Yoesting** backs Sam.*

Source: Article by Travis Yoesting, The 18, August 7, 2021, the18.com

---

#TedLasso new episode is truly a standout this season. It'll have you falling even more in love with Sam Obisanya, and leave you thinking about its message long after you've watched it.

Aiko Hilkinger *on Season 2 Episode 3.*

Source: Twitter, August 7, 2021

BELIEVE

66

Sam is, essentially, a good guy whose dad raised him right and cultivated in him a taste for reading and Disney's animation catalogue.

99

Melanie McFarland *on the basics of what makes Sam an interesting character.*

Source: Melanie McFarland in *Salon*, September 25, 2021, salon.com

---

ISAAC MCADOO
(Kola Bokinni)

Kola wale Anthony Bokinni was born in London, England, and he grew up in Peckham. He went to the BRIT school of performing arts and has been acting since he was 14.

He was in *100 Streets* (with Idris Elba) in 2016 and has appeared in *Top Boy*, *Black Mirror*, and *Cursed*.

BELIEVE

66

I came up with the construct that Isaac only thinks of one thought at a time. He only has space for one thought at a time. **99**

Kola Bokinni provides insight to Isaac McAdoo's character makeup.

Source: Article by Meredith B. Kile in *ET*, October 8, 2021, etonline.com

---

I read, 'Can play football and act.' And I was just like, 'Wait, hold on a second. Someone's made this up. Someone's just trying to trick me. Football was my life, before acting.'

Kola Bokinni *on finding joy on* Ted Lasso*.*

Source: Article by Meredith B. Kile in *ET*, October 8, 2021, etonline.com

COLIN HUGHES

(Billy Harris)

Billy Harris is an English actor who has also appeared in various other television shows, including *Something's Wrong* in 2015 and *Heart of Nowhere* in 2013.

66

It kind of dropped during lockdown so I just think everyone needed— and even I think I needed it.

99

Billy Harris on the amazing critic and public reaction to Ted Lasso.

Source: Interview with Chris Hue, Popternative, September 2, 2021, popternative.com

RICHARD MONTLAUR
(Stephen Manas)

Born in Saint-Germain-en-Laye, France, in 1982, Stephen studied at the University of Paris 1 Pantheon-Sorbonne.

He began acting in 2010 and spend time in India, Japan, and the Philippines honing his craft before a return to Europe. He won awards for his work in the short film *Out of Frame* in 2019, and he has played various roles in France.

I don't think they had any idea of what nationality it should be. Instead, the casting call just specified that they were looking for someone who was young and 'not English.'

Stephen Manas *on how the character of Richard came to be in* Ted Lasso.

Source: Interview with Ashley Bissette Sumerel, Tell-Tale TV, July 23, 2001, telltaletv.com

BELIEVE

66

He's very good in football, but
he doesn't have a lot of cohesion
with the team.

99

Stephen Manas *on his character Richard's
integration with AFC Richmond.*

Source: Interview with Lance Carter, *Daily Actor*,
July 26, 2021, dailyactor.com

I like this character. He's a little like me. Quite simple, honest, and he loves having fun.

Stephen Manas *on Richard Montlaur's similarities with the actor who portrays him.*

Source: Interview with Ashley Bissette Sumerel, Tell-Tale TV, July 23, 2001, telltaletv.com

THIERRY ZOREAUX

(Moe Jeudy-Lamour)

Moe was born in Montreal, Canada.
His television work includes
Unité 9, *Les Jeunes Loups*, *Incorporated*,
Bad Blood, and *Victor Lessard*.

He was on the big screen in
Immortals, *X-Men: Days of Future Past*,
and *Race*.

DANI ROJAS
(Cristo FernÁndez)

Born in Mexico, Cristo originally trained for a career in soccer until he was sidelined by an injury. Then he took up acting, specifically film classes, and he worked to pay his way through further eduction and schooling.

BELIEVE

❝

I think *Ted Lasso* has allowed me to realize the importance of sending a message, whatever it is, just put something there that has a core and has a heart.

❞

Cristo Fernández *on his discovery of the significance of* Ted Lasso.

Source: Interview with Sandra Gonzales, CNN, July 22, 2021, edition.cnn.com

---

I thank my parents for encouraging me to try something new, and that's what I also encourage everyone in life [to do]. They should never close themselves to other opportunities.

Cristo Fernández on his *positive parental influence*.

Source: Interview with Sandra Gonzales, CNN, July 22, 2021, edition.cnn.com

BELIEVE

66

Football is life!

99

> **Dani Rojas** is very clear about
> his philosophy.

Source: Quoted in "When a Show about Kindness Gets
Darker" by Megan Garber, *The Atlantic*, July 23, 2021,
theatlantic.com

WILL KITMAN
(Charlie J. Hiscock)

Charlie started acting at the age of nine and has been in the BAFTA-award-winning show *Secret Life of Boys* and BBC's *The Borrowers*.

BELIEVE

66

I came into the show not knowing
what to expect!

99

Charlie Hiscock *on his joining* Ted Lasso
for Season 2.

Source: Interview with Lauren Castro, *Flaunt*,
August 6, 2021, flaunt.com

So when the world was very down and ill and needed someone/thing to rely on and have that bit of warmth in the heart again, *Ted Lasso* came along and did just that in the most unexpected surprise.

Charlie Hiscock *on the* Ted Lasso *effect.*

Source: Interview with Lauren Castro, *Flaunt*, August 6, 2021, flaunt.com

JAN MAAS
(David Elsendoorn)

David was born in Groningen
in Holland and graduated from the
Amsterdam Toneelschool in 2018.

He was in the television series
Ik Went Wie Je Bent, *SpangaS*,
and *Turbulent Skies*, and the movie
Gelukszoekers.

We make the series with such a special group of people, and I feel immensely privileged and incredibly grateful to be able to learn from such fantastic professionals. They are all such inspiring actors.

David Elsendoorn *provides insight into his* Ted Lasso *colleagues.*

Source: David Elsendoorn quoted in *NL Times*, September 20, 2021, nltimes.nl

BELIEVE

66

All the time I was on set I really wanted to share it with the world.

99

David Elsendoorn on the excitement of filming Season 2.

Source: Interview with Chris Hue, Popternative, August 27, 2021, popternative.com

---

TRENT CRIMM
(James Lance)

James Lance was born in 1974 in Southampton, England. He has appeared in many television shows, including *I'm Alan Partridge*, *Spaced*, *Absolutely Fabulous*, *Smack the Pony*, *Teachers*, *Boy Meets Girl*, *Marple*, *Black Mirror*, and *Midsomer Murders*.

He has also appeared in a number of movies, including *Late Night Shopping*, *Marie Antoinette*, and *Bel Ami*.

BELIEVE

66

If the Lasso way is wrong, it's hard to imagine being right.

99

Trent Crimm, of The Independent, *warms to Ted Lasso and his methods.*

Source: Quoted by Katie Bowlby, *Country Living*, August 24, 2021, countryliving.com

---

Trent Crimm: It's a lovely novel. It's the story of a young girl's struggle with the burden of leadership as she journeys through space.

Ted: Yeah. That's it.

Roy: Am I supposed to be the little girl?

Ted: I'd like you to be.

Trent Crimm, of The Independent, *helps Roy Kent discover literature.*

Source: Quoted in "Overanalyzing Every Book in *Ted Lasso* to Predict Season 2" by Danika Ellis, May 19, 2021, book riot.com

MAE
(Annette Badland)

Annette is an English actress, born
in Edgbaston, Birmingham, in 1950.
She has had a vast, varied career
in acting, including theater, radio,
television, and film.

Her television credits include
Outlander, *EastEnders*, *The Sparticle
Mystery*, and many, many more.

"

It's the hope that kills you.

"

Mae's very British outlook on supporting soccer causes Ted some problems.

Source: Quoted by Daniel Hart, Ready Steady Cut, October 2, 2020, readysteadycut.com

THE REAL DEAL

Players, commentators, and other real people who have appeared on *Ted Lasso* as themselves:

Jeff Stelling • Scott Van Pelt

Arlo White • Chris Powell

Eni Aluko • Chris Kamara

Thierry Henry • Gary Lineker

Ian Wright • Mike Dean

Peter Crouch • Fleur East

Seema Jaswal • Holly Willoughby

IN THE BOOK

There are many literary themes in *Ted Lasso*, and books play an important role, including:

A Wrinkle in Time (Madeleine L'Engle)

One Flew over the Cuckoo's Nest (Ken Kesey)

The Beautiful and the Damned (F. Scott Fitzgerald)

The Ultimate Cockney Geezer's Guide to Rhyming Slang (Geoff Tibballs)

The Dharma Bums (Jack Kerouac)

The Da Vinci Code (Dan Brown)

Inverting the Pyramid: The History of Soccer Tactics (Jonathan Wilson)

Football against the Enemy (Simon Kuper)

Ender's Game (Orson Scott Card)

Coach Wooden's Pyramid of Success (John Wooden and Jay Party)

BELIEVE

Ted: Back home if a team was playing poorly we don't call them unlucky. What do we call 'em, coach?
Coach Beard: New York Jets!

Geoff Magliocchetti

Source: Quoted in "*Ted Lasso* Roasts New York Jets in Season 2 Trailer" by Geoff Magliocchetti, Jet X, April 20, 2021, jetsxfactor.com

CHAPTER

3

EXPLAIN OFFSIDE TO ME

Ted Lasso is all about soccer
(OK, football) ... Or is it?

Although sport is the platform,
the real subject of the series is
people, their fears, dreams, hopes,
relationships, and failings.

But it is also about
football (soccer).

I think I literally have a better understanding of who killed Kennedy than what is offside.

Ted Lasso on the basics of the offside rule.

Source: Quoted by Brianne Hogan,
October 24, 2021, scarymommy.com

BELIEVE

> **"**
> Come on, now! What do you mean? How's that offside? ... No, I'm serious. How's that offside ... I don't understand it yet. **"**

(Premier League Coach) **Ted Lasso** *demonstrates his knowledge of the offside rule.*

Source: Quoted in article by Luis Miguel Echegaray, *Sports Illustrated*, August 11, 2020, si.com

All right, fellas, you gotta remember, your body is like day-old rice. If it ain't warmed up properly, something real bad could happen.

Ted Lasso relates food to food-eaters.

Source: Quoted by Brianne Hogan,
October 24, 2021, scarymommy.com

BELIEVE

The soccer comedy is its folksy, charming self in season two. That might be why some people are so mad at it.

Critic **Emily VanDerWerff**
on the continuing success of Ted Lasso.

Source: "The *Ted Lasso* Backlash Was Inevitable" by Emily VanDerWerff, August 31, 2021, vox.com

---

66

If God would have wanted games to end in a tie, she wouldn't have invented numbers. **99**

An insight into **Ted Lasso**'s ideas on the *Almighty*.

Source: Quoted by Brianne Hogan, October 24, 2021, scarymommy.com

---

BELIEVE

66

Pressure makes pearls, right?

99

Ted Lasso on how to get the best out of
people, especially the team.

Source: Quoted by Tania Lamb in Lola Lambchops,
October 8, 2021, lolalambchops.com

"

I want you to know, I value each of your opinions, even when you're wrong.

"

Ted Lasso demonstrates his balanced views.

Source: Quoted by Brianne Hogan,
October 24, 2021, scarymommy.com

BELIEVE

❝

The second season features five or six conflicts that are at a simmer, just waiting to boil over. It's very well-crafted and, in general, I have found it to be a marked improvement on season one.

❞

Critic **Emily VanDerWerff**
on the continuing success of Ted Lasso.

Source: "The *Ted Lasso* Backlash Was Inevitable" by Emily
VanDerWerff, August 31, 2021, vox.com

Ties and no playoffs? Why do you even do this?

Ted Lasso's American sporting sensitivities are challenged.

Source: Quoted by Brianne Hogan, October 24, 2021, scarymommy.com

---

BELIEVE

"

By the end of *Ted Lasso*'s first episode, the show that kept so many of us going has found its feet and is racing up the league tables towards its rightful place once more.

"

*Critic **Lucy Mangan** on Season 2.*

Source: Lucy Mangan review in *The Guardian*, July 23, 2020, theguardian.com

---

66

Our goal is to go out like Willie Nelson—on a high!

99

Ted Lasso refers to the country-and-western star.

Source: Quoted by Josh Jackson article in *Paste*, November 3, 2021, pastemagazine.com

---

BELIEVE

"

I've become a fan of LAFC, they're my team, I root for them. But every time that I'm at the game and the opposing goalkeeper does a nice save, I have to cheer. I'm a fan of goalkeepers now: That's my thing. I'll always watch them. **"**

__Moe Jeudy-Lamour__ on his new outlook on watching soccer.

Source: Interview with Emily Burack, *Alma*, September 17, 2021, heyalma.com

---

WHO'S FOOLING WHO

Various members of the cast attended the FA Cup final at Wembley Stadium in May 2021 including Sam, Jamie, Isaac, Dani, Colin, and Richard.

They were interviewed by unsuspecting ITV reporter Chris Skudder and even sang a round of "Na-na-na-na-na-na-na-na-na-na-na-Dani Rojas!"

BELIEVE

> **"**
> Unceasing optimism defines *Ted Lasso*. But roller-coaster mood storms, manic reveries, and seemingly deliberate head games also define Ted Lasso, the players' coach, and make him one of the best and most-layered characters of the peak TV era. **"**

*Critic **Elizabeth Nelson** celebrating the character that is Ted Lasso.*

Source: "What Lies Beneath Ted Lasso" by Elizabeth Nelson in *The Ringer*, July 21, 2021, theringer.com

Dr. Fieldstone deals in truth, and over the season she is the catalyst for growth in Ted in ways that stay true both to him and to the show's comic, tender spirit.

Lucy Mangan *on the Dr. Fieldstone effect in Season 2.*

Source: Lucy Mangan review in *The Guardian*, July 23, 2020, theguardian.com

BELIEVE

> **"**
> Our coach is khakied, mustachioed, and heavily accented. Like Ned Flanders, he works with an almost religious determination. **"**

Doreen St. Félix compares Ted Lasso to Homer Simpson's neighbor.

Source: *The New Yorker*, August 9, 2021, newyorker.com

AWARDS SEASON

Not only is *Ted Lasso* a fan favorite, but it won a stonking seven awards at the 2021 Emmys, including three outstanding actor categories, oustanding comedy series, casting, picture editing, and sound mixing.

The show's 20 nominations was a new record for a comedy series. *Ted Lasso* also won many other awards in 2021, including Critics' Choice, Hollywood Critics Association, MTV, and a Golden Globe.

BELIEVE

66

Sam was more open than the jar of
peanut butter on my counter. **99**

Ted Lasso on Obisanya's on-field positioning.

Source: Quoted by Katie Bowlby, *Country Living*,
August 24, 2021, countryliving.com

I don't know how I'd feel, I mean, to go to Emirates, to touch the grass, would be a dream, for both me and Brendan [Hunt], who are devout fans.

Kola Bokinni on the thought of AFC Richmond playing Arsenal FC.

Source: Article by Meredith B. Kile in *ET*, October 8, 2021, etonline.com

BELIEVE

"

I love watching it. I love watching the clubs. I love watching Ajax with my friends.

"

David Elsendoorn *on how much he likes soccer (football, if you will).*

Source: Interview with Chris Hue, Popternative, August 27, 2021, popternative.com

---

With *Ted Lasso*, the football didn't really seem to matter as much. The message is more important.

Billy Harris *on the show's real meaning.*

Source: Interview with Chris Hue, Popternative, September 2, 2021, popternative.com

---

66

Zoreaux: Midnight Poutine!
Lasso: Poutine?
Coach Beard: That's not dirty, it's just super Canadian.

99

Zoreaux, *Lasso*, *and* *Coach Beard* *discuss a new set-piece routine.*

Source: Quoted in interview with Douglas Gelevan, CBC News, September 6, 2021, cbc.ca

---

> Coach Beard remains as gloriously gnomic as ever. He means everything to me. I would die for him.

*Critic **Lucy Mangan** on the talents of Ted Lasso's coaching staff (some of them).*

Source: Lucy Mangan in *The Guardian*,
July 23, 2020, theguardian.com

BELIEVE

66

Every time I go to see a match,
I buy a kit for me at the gift shop
and a kit for my little boy. I'm
ready to be a fair-weather fan for
whoever needs it. **99**

Jason Sudeikis *on supporting
a soccer team IRL.*

Source: Article by Luis Miguel Echegaray, *Sports Illustrated*,
August 11, 2020, si.com

CHAPTER

4

HOT BROWN WATER

To say Ted Lasso was a fish out of water would be an understatement. He sticks out like a marlin flapping in a dustbowl and his cultural references, background, experiences, and language all mark him as an outsider.

But with a whole language in common, how difficult can it be ...

Last one there is a Scotch egg.

Ted Lasso gets his metaphors muddled when training the team.

Source: Quoted by Tania Lamb in Lola Lambchops, October 8, 2021, lolalambchops.com

---

BELIEVE

"

I think it means great. Best guy. Kind heart. You know, someone that listens, someone that'll push ya, a wanker is someone who doesn't mind being alone. You know, likes to sit with his thoughts.

"

__Ted Lasso__ on his rather quaint (mis)understanding of the word "wanker."

Source: Quoted by Grant Marek, article on SFGATE, August 2, 2021, sfgate.com

---

I always figured that tea was just gonna taste like hot brown water. And you know what? I was right. Yeah, it's horrible.

***Ted Lasso** passes judgment on the U.K.'s favorite drink.*

Source: Quoted by Evelina Zaragoza Medina, BuzzFeed, October 17, 2021, buzzfeed.com

---

BELIEVE

66

If that's a joke, I love it. If not, can't wait to unpack that with you later.

99

Ted on Rebecca's comment about her father.

Source: Quoted by Katie Bowlby, *Country Living*,
August 24, 2021, countryliving.com

66

Tea is horrible. Absolute garbage water. I don't know why y'all do that. **99**

Ted Lasso *passes judgment on the U.K.'s favorite drink, #2.*

Source: Quoted by Evelina Zaragoza Medina, BuzzFeed, October 17, 2021, buzzfeed.com

---

BELIEVE

❝
That right there, that's a scone.
Tastes like a muffin except it sucks
all the spit out of your mouth. **❞**

Ted Lasso *on a British culinary institution.*

Source: Quoted by Brianne Hogan,
October 24, 2021, scarymommy.com

❝

As the man once said, the harder you work, the luckier you get.

❞

Ted Lasso *on his carefully researched training philosophy.*

Source: Quoted by Katie Bowlby, *Country Living*, August 24, 2021, countryliving.com

---

BELIEVE

"

Be honest with me. It's a prank, right? The tea? Like when us tourist folks aren't around, y'all know it tastes like garbage? You don't love it.

"

__Ted Lasso__ passes judgment on the U.K.'s favorite drink, #3.

Source: Quoted by Evelina Zaragoza Medina, BuzzFeed, October 17, 2021, buzzfeed.com

---

We're gonna call this drill 'The Exorcist' 'cause it's all about controlling possession.

Ted Lasso really does have an analogy for everything.

Source: Quoted by Evelina Zaragoza Medina, BuzzFeed, October 17, 2021, buzzfeed.com

BELIEVE

―――――――――――

"

Tea and I are still on a lifelong hiatus.

"

Ted Lasso passes judgment on the U.K.'s favorite drink, #4.

Source: Quoted by Brianne Hogan,
October 24, 2021, scarymommy.com

―――――――――――

66

I'm gonna put it the same way the U.S. Supreme Court did back in 1964 when they defined pornography. It ain't easy to explain, but you know it when you see it.

99

Ted Lasso on the offside rule once again.

Source: Quoted by Evelina Zaragoza Medina, BuzzFeed, October 17, 2021, buzzfeed.com

BELIEVE

66

You are more mysterious than David Blaine reading a Sue Grafton novel at Area 51.

99

Ted Lasso loves a challenge.

Source: Quoted by Josh Jackson article in *Paste*, November 3, 2021, pastemagazine.com

---

CHAPTER

5

ONE IN ELEVEN

Ted Lasso is an amazingly inspirational coach. He always finds a way; he always has an insight, an experience, or an example to cheer, chivvy, and chase his team to greatness. This chapter looks at some of Ted's finest moments, as well as the cast's reactions to the writing, filming, and success of the show.

When it comes to locker rooms, I like 'em just like my mother's bathing suits. I only wanna see 'em in one piece, you hear.

***Ted Lasso** reveals a little more about his upbringing and his morals.*

Source: Quoted by Evelina Zaragoza Medina, BuzzFeed, October 17, 2021, buzzfeed.com

BELIEVE

"

I think that you might be so sure that you're one in a million … sometimes you forget that out there, you're just one of 11. And if you just figure out some way to turn that me into us, whew—sky's the limit for you.

"

Ted Lasso's inspirational talk to Jamie Tartt. Jamie goes back to Manchester City shortly afterwards.

Source: Quoted in "When a Show about Kindness Gets Darker" by Megan Garber, *The Atlantic*, July 23, 2021, theatlantic.com

> 66
>
> Here's an idea that's gonna help a little or hurt a whole lot: Who needs a drink? 99

Ted Lasso with one of his less conventional coaching methods.

Source: Quoted by Evelina Zaragoza Medina, BuzzFeed, October 17, 2021, buzzfeed.com

BELIEVE

66

Heck, you could fill two
internets with what I don't know
about football.

99

Ted Lasso *reveals an early sign of honesty at
his first press conference.*

Source: Quoted in *Ted Lasso* review, *Entertainment Weekly*,
August 3, 2021, ew.com

Taking on a challenge is a lot like riding a horse, isn't it? If you're comfortable while you're doing it, you're probably doing it wrong.

Ted Lasso *on his new management task.*

Source: Quoted by Evelina Zaragoza Medina, BuzzFeed, October 17, 2021, buzzfeed.com

---

BELIEVE

66

You deserve someone who makes you feel like you've been struck by fucking lightning. Don't you dare settle for fine.

99

Roy Kane reveals his—admittedly well hidden—romantic side.

Source: Quoted by Josh Jackson article in *Paste*, November 3, 2021, pastemagazine.com

---

For me, success is not about the wins and losses. It's about helping these young fellas be the best versions of themselves on and off the field.

Ted Lasso on his definition of how to make it in the Premier League.

Source: Quoted in "When a Show about Kindness Gets Darker" by Megan Garber, *The Atlantic*, July 23, 2021, theatlantic.com

---

BELIEVE

66

So then, next year we get ourselves a promotion, which looks good on any résumé. Then we come back to this league and … we do something that no one believes we could ever do: Win the whole fucking thing.

99

Ted Lasso on promotion after relegation [Also a Tom Berenger line in Major League].

Source: Quoted in "What Lies Beneath Ted Lasso" by Elizabeth Nelson in *The Ringer*, July 21, 2021, theringer.com

> **"**
>
> It's basically happiest animal in the world is a goldfish. You know why? He's got a ten-second memory. I played great golf last week, just a couple bad swings down the stretch, and that's the most important thing to remember. **"**

*Golfer **Jon Rahm** channels his inner Ted Lasso.*

Source: "Jon Rahm Says 'Ted Lasso' Could Make You a Better Golfer—Here's How" by Dylan Dethier in *Golf*, August 27, 2021, golf.com

BELIEVE

66

Be a goldfish.

99

Ted Lasso's advice to Sam.

Source: "The History of Ted Lasso" by Arul Gnanasivam,
DBK News, September 22, 2021, dbknews.com

The only person I've seen lose their man more often is Carrie fucking Bradshaw.

Nate *makes a* Sex and the City *reference to Dani Rojas.*

Source: Quoted in "Overanalyzing Every Book in *Ted Lasso* to Predict Season 2" by Danika Ellis, May 19, 2021, book riot.com

BELIEVE

66

No, no, no. This is a no-schadenfreude zone.

99

*Ted to Nate, on Jamie Tartt being
put in his place.*

Source: Quoted in Bill Lawrence interview with Josh Jackson,
Paste, October 2, 2020, pastemagazine.com

You beating yourself up is like Woody Allen playing the clarinet. I don't want to hear it.

Ted Lasso on self-deprecation.

Source: Quoted by Brianne Hogan,
October 24, 2021, scarymommy.com

BELIEVE

"

Old people are so wise. They're like tall Yodas.

"

Jamie Tartt's Star Wars *frame of reference is somewhat transparent.*

Source: Quoted by Josh Jackson article in *Paste*, November 3, 2021, pastemagazine.com

---

———————————————————————

66

Coach, I'm me. Why would I want
to be anything else?

99

Jamie Tartt has no self-esteem issues.

Source: Quoted by Kristen Kranz in Hypable,
April 8, 2021, hypable.com

———————————————————————

BELIEVE

66

I feel like we all have conversations that reflects the kind of masculinity that is portrayed on the screen in *Ted Lasso*.

99

Charlie Hiscock *(Will Kitman) on the new maleness seen in* Ted Lasso.

Source: Interview with Lauren Castro, *Flaunt*, August 6, 2021, flaunt.com

---

Oh, no, no, no, no. I have five boys. I never look over anyone's shoulders to see what's on their screens.

Higgins has learned by bitter experience.

Source: Quoted by Josh Jackson article in *Paste*, November 3, 2021, pastemagazine.com

BELIEVE

66

Little girls are mysterious. And silly and powerful. I gave up trying to figure them out years ago. 99

*There are some things that even **Ted Lasso** cannot understand.*

Source: Quoted by Kristen Kranz in Hypable, April 8, 2021, hypable.com

You're nearly 70, and you're having a baby? I mean, what are you, a character from the fucking Bible?

Rebecca to ex-husband *Rupert* on the announcment of his impending heir.

Source: Quoted by Josh Jackson article in *Paste*, November 3, 2021, pastemagazine.com

WRITING ON THE WALL

Posters at AFC Richmond:

BELIEVE

Gradarius Firmus Victoria

#WE ARE RICHMOND

Just Keep Trying

Winners Don't Quit; Quitters Don't Win

CHAPTER

6

I BELIEVE IN BELIEVE

Ted Lasso deals with many simple-but-complex issues. Launching in the middle of the Covid-19 pandemic, it became a roaring success and swept up at the awards season soon after.

The reason? Despite a gruff exterior and plenty of shouting and swearing, *Ted Lasso* is a heartwarming, positive take on people, relationships, love, and understanding.

I mean, the writers are fabulous. You got some heavyweights there, so I kind of leave it up to them. I think they know what they're doing with Isaac, and I trust them completely.

Kola Bokinni *on the making of* Ted Lasso.

Source: Article by Meredith B. Kile in ET, October 8, 2021, etonline.com

BELIEVE

66

It's sad to say, but it was perfect timing that it came out at the height of the pandemic and everybody needed a hug and the show was basically a big hug.

99

Moe Jeudy-Lamour *on the importance and positivity of* Ted Lasso.

Source: Interview with Douglas Gelevan, CBC News, September 6, 2021, cbc.ca

The only way I think a fourth season of *Ted Lasso* exists would be if Ted Lasso went and coached a soccer team that played about a block from Jason's house in real life, you know what I mean.

Bill Lawrence *(co-creator of Ted Lasso) on the show's long-term future.*

Source: Fake Doctors, Real Friends podcast, quoted in "The Heartbreaking Truth about 'Ted Lasso' Season 2 and the Show's Future" by Kayla Keegan, *Good Housekeeping*, June 6, 2021, goodhousekeeping.com

BELIEVE

66

I believe in hope. I believe in
BELIEVE.

99

Ted Lasso has unbelievable belief.

Source: Quoted by Kristen Kranz in Hypable,
April 8, 2021, hypable.com

66

Ted Lasso has no right to be this funny.

99

Critic **Kristen Baldwin**.

Source: *Ted Lasso* review, *Entertainment Weekly*, August 3, 2021, ew.com

BELIEVE

66

I think a really good message
of our show is to get rid of
this macho mentality and the
unhealthy masculinity where men
don't cry, men don't speak about
their feelings.

99

*Cristo Fernández (Dani Rojas) on the show's
contribution to mental health and maleness.*

Source: Interview with Sandra Gonzales, CNN,
July 22, 2021, edition.cnn.com

> Through a feel-good story about a soccer team, *Ted Lasso* slyly questions Americans' abiding mythologies—about talent, about success, about the elemental relationship between the individual interest and the collective good.

*Critic **Megan Garber** on what the show is really about.*

Source: "When a Show about Kindness Gets Darker" by Megan Garber, *The Atlantic*, July 23, 2021, theatlantic.com

BELIEVE

> **66**
>
> I gotta say, man, sometimes you remind me of my grandma with the channel hopper. You just push all the wrong buttons. **99**

Ted Lasso *with an another fresh analogy.*

Source: Quoted by Evelina Zaragoza Medina, BuzzFeed, October 17, 2021, buzzfeed.com

I think he'd be thriving. I mean, he makes the best of a bad situation. He's an indomitable spirit.

Jason Sudeikis *on how Ted would get through the Coronavirus pandemic.*

Source: Interview with Derek Lawrence in *Entertainment Weekly*, August 13, 2020, ew.com

BELIEVE

"

We try to still keep the joy and the goal of believing in everything we're doing.

"

Stephen Manas *on the team and the future of* Ted Lasso.

Source: Interview with Ashley Bissette Sumerel, Tell-Tale TV, July 23, 2001, telltaletv.com

---

This show came out at time when the world needed a big hug and I'd like to say that the show was the TV version of a big warm hug.

Charlie Hiscock *on the positive message behind* Ted Lasso.

Source: Interview with Lauren Castro, *Flaunt*, August 6, 2021, flaunt.com

BELIEVE

❝

If the internet has taught us anything, it's that sometimes it's easier to speak our minds anonymously.

❞

Ted Lasso comments on today's popular methods of communication and criticism.

Source: Quoted by Katie Bowlby, *Country Living,* August 24, 2021, countryliving.com

---

He's more white rabbit than white knight, but he's actually becoming the change he wants to see in the world, without any agenda. And these days, that's unusual, both in real life and on television.

Jason Sudeikis *on the meaning of Ted Lasso's character.*

Source: Article by Luis Miguel Echegaray, *Sports Illustrated*, August 11, 2020, si.com

BELIEVE

" 'There's two buttons I never like hitting. That's panic, and snooze.' I love that. I love that.

"

Apple CEO **Tim Cook** *on his favorite line from* Ted Lasso.

Source: Tim Cook quoted from the *New York Times* DealBook Online Summit by Jill Goldsmith, Deadline, November 9, 2021, deadline.com

Ted admits that his defining selflessness, to be fully effective, requires him to take care of himself. A soccer team moves, together, down the field, passing the ball, navigating the obstacles. Their mistakes are shared, as are their victories.

*Critic **Megan Garber** on Ted, the team and Season 2.*

Source: "When a Show about Kindness Gets Darker" by Megan Garber, *The Atlantic*, July 23, 2021, theatlantic.com

BELIEVE

66

We delight in his antics, marinate in his charm offensive, and celebrate his offbeat approach to winning the whole fucking thing. But at all times, there's a slight worry, one that crops up in the back of our minds, about what he might be willing to do to make it happen.

99

*Critic **Elizabeth Nelson** wonders about the darker side of Ted.*

Source: Quoted in "What Lies Beneath Ted Lasso" by Elizabeth Nelson in *The Ringer*, July 21, 2021, theringer.com

Boy, I love meeting people's moms. It's like reading an instruction manual as to why they're nuts.

Ted Lasso *with a way to get the therapy started.*

Source: Quoted by Josh Jackson article in *Paste*, November 3, 2021, pastemagazine.com